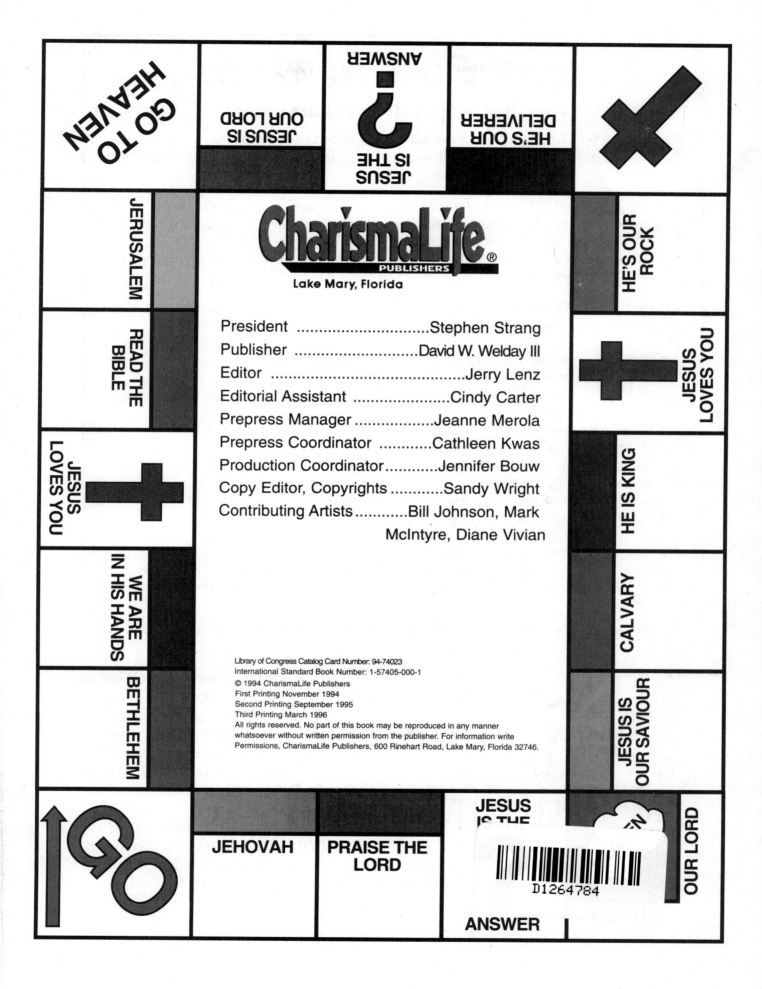

GO TO HEAVEN

JESUS IS OUR LORD

ANSWER
¿
JESUS IS THE

HE'S OUR DELIVERER

✗

JERUSALEM

HE'S OUR ROCK

READ THE BIBLE

✚ JESUS LOVES YOU

JESUS LOVES YOU ✚

HE IS KING

WE ARE IN HIS HANDS

CALVARY

BETHLEHEM

JESUS IS OUR SAVIOUR

GO ⬆

JEHOVAH

PRAISE THE LORD

JESUS IS THE ... ANSWER

OUR LORD

CharismaLife
PUBLISHERS ®
Lake Mary, Florida

President ....Stephen Strang
Publisher ....David W. Welday III
Editor ....Jerry Lenz
Editorial Assistant ....Cindy Carter
Prepress Manager ....Jeanne Merola
Prepress Coordinator ....Cathleen Kwas
Production Coordinator............Jennifer Bouw
Copy Editor, Copyrights ....Sandy Wright
Contributing Artists............Bill Johnson, Mark
                             McIntyre, Diane Vivian

Library of Congress Catalog Card Number: 94-74023
International Standard Book Number: 1-57405-000-1

© 1994 CharismaLife Publishers
First Printing November 1994
Second Printing September 1995
Third Printing March 1996

Power Pak of Games

Compiled by the editors of KIDS Church

Kids often ask, **Do Christians have fun?** They need to know that going to church can actually be enjoyable. That's why we believe in using GAMES to accomplish three specific goals:

1. Games can set the tone for the rest of the service. Start out on a positive note.
2. Games are great fidget busters. Kids need to release some energy before settling into the more serious aspects of church.
3. Games can be a great evangelistic tool. If your kids look forward to coming to church, they'll be sure to invite their friends!

Power Pak of Games offers 100 exciting and fun-filled games divided into eight exhilarating categories. Here are some tips for making your games more effective:

▼ Test the game before using it so there will be no surprises.
▼ Situate the games so everyone can see. A stage is best.
▼ Use a microphone to your advantage. Talk continuously during the game—there should be no dead air time.
▼ Let your workers set up games and explain them clearly to all players.
▼ Use a whistle as a means for signaling QUIET!
▼ Background music helps to generate excitement. Use a live band or play upbeat cassettes during the games.
▼ Get the audience cheering—keep them enthusiastic.
▼ Avoid repeating popular games too frequently.

Use your games to encourage learning. When it's time for preaching, tell the kids that only those who can answer the review questions the following week will have a chance to play. Then choose your contestants after a quick review session at the start of your next program.

Games can be a powerful and exciting addition to your children's church program. We have developed a full-line of wonderful children's church programs called KIDS Church (Kids In Divine Service).

If you'd like more information about these resources, contact your local Christian bookstore or call us at 1-800-451-4598.

TABLE OF CONTENTS

Action Games

GO TO HEAVEN	JESUS IS OUR LORD	JESUS IS THE ANSWER	HE'S OUR DELIVERER	✗
JERUSALEM				HE'S OUR ROCK
READ THE BIBLE				JESUS LOVES YOU ✝
JESUS LOVES YOU ✝				HE IS KING
WE ARE IN HIS HANDS				CALVARY
BETHLEHEM				JESUS IS OUR SAVIOUR
GO ↑	JEHOVAH	PRAISE THE LORD	JESUS IS THE ? ANSWER	HEAVEN BE WITH OUR LORD

● START

Musical Hats

PROPS: 5 loose-fitting hats (army helmets, large bowls, or even Kentucky Fried Chicken® buckets) and musical instrument (or cassette and cassette player).

PARTICIPANTS: 6 children.

H ave participants form a circle facing in the same direction. Explain the game will work just like musical chairs, only they will be using hats.

As the music starts, each person will place his hat on the head of the person in front of him. They need to do this quickly until the music stops. When the music stops, they hold onto the hat they have. The person without a hat will sit down. Take away one hat, and make the circle smaller. Continue this until there are only two people left. Have them face each other. When they place the hat on each other's head, they must remove their hands from the hat so two people aren't simultaneously holding the hat. The person with the hat on his head when the music stops is the winner.

Be sure to practice with the kids before the game starts. This can be difficult for some younger ones, and they will need to have an idea of how the game goes before they start.

YOU ARE HERE

START

Beach Ball Bash

PROPS: 2 giant beach balls.

PARTICIPANTS: 1 boy and 1 girl to be team leaders.

Have the audience participate in the game. First, review the rules with them:

1. Everyone remains seated.

2. No standing.

3. Keep hands to yourself.

4. Hit only the beach ball.

The team leaders start by throwing their balls to their teams. The teams volley the balls from the front to the back of the room and then volley the balls back to the front and to their leaders.

If the ball is dropped, the team loses. The winning team is the one that works best together and returns the ball to their leader first.

Allow both teams two or three tries and award points based on their performance. Promote cheering and enthusiasm for the teams to encourage one another.

● START

PROPS: 2 large shirts, 10 balloons and tape.

PARTICIPANTS: 2 children.

Before the service starts, tape 10 balloons to each shirt (five to the front of each shirt and five to the back of each shirt).

As the two participants come to the front, put the shirts on them. The object of the game is to see which participant can pop all the balloons on her shirt first. They can squeeze them, bite them, roll on the ground, or pinch them. The first person to finish stands up and puts her hands in the air.

READY! SET! GO! Begin the game. Reward the winner with a small prize or piece of candy.

HINT

Use small balloons blown all the way up instead of large balloons blown halfway up. The larger balloons will be very hard to pop. Have a few extra balloons with tape on them in case a balloon pops before the game starts.

YOU ARE HERE

● START

PLAYING

PROPS: 20 six-packs of soda.

PARTICIPANTS: Everyone in the service, divided into 2 teams, in a line on each side of the room.

Line up the two teams on opposite sides of the room. Put ten six-packs at the back end of each line of players. At the start of the game, the last person in each line will pick up a six-pack and hand it to the person in front of him, who will hand it to the person in front of him, and so on. As the first six-pack is being passed forward, the last person will begin passing the second six-pack up, then the third, fourth, fifth, etc. The first person in the line will take the six-pack as he gets it and begin a stack *(Have them stack the whole six-pack, not individual cans.)* The first team to pass all their six-packs to the front and have them in one stack wins.

YOU ARE HERE

HINT

Only allow the children to hold one six-pack at a time. If they try to double-up, they will probably end up dropping the sodas.

● **START** -

Swim Fin Jump Rope

PROPS: 2 jump ropes, 2 sets of swim fins and stopwatch (or watch with a second hand).

PARTICIPANTS: 2 children and 2 helpers (adults or older kids) to count.

Put the swim fins on the kids, and give each of them a jump rope. Have a helper for each kid count the number of times they make a complete jump. Whoever makes the most jumps in one minute wins. This game is hilarious to watch as the kids desperately try to do something simple that turns into quite a task with the swim fins.

YOU ARE HERE

Before the game actually starts, have children take one or two practice jumps to get a feel for what they need to do.

● **START**

PROPS: 6 rolls of toilet paper ("T.P.") and stopwatch (or watch with second hand).

PARTICIPANTS: 6 children.

The object is to totally wrap you, the Children's Pastor ("C.P."), with toilet paper! Of course, you'll want a trusted worker or leader to carefully time this event to last only 60 seconds. Have the six kids come to the front of the room and hand each of them a roll of toilet paper. You will sit on the floor, and your worker will then tell the children that at the count of three they will have only 60 seconds to "T.P. the C.P." Your worker counts to three and says, "Go!" At 60 seconds, she tells them to stop. (If she's really your friend!)

YOU ARE HERE

The children will enjoy this activity even more if you squirm around, vocally protest and generally "act" as if you are not enjoying yourself!

If done properly, "mummy style," it is quite likely that you will not be able to walk or move your arms to remove the "T.P." Have a trusted worker help you unwrap the toilet paper. Also, be prepared to clean up approximately 3,000 to 6,000 feet of "T.P."!

● START

Toy Stuff

PROPS: Large cloth duffel (or similar bag), large assortment of many different kinds of small- to medium-sized toys (more than will fit in the bag), stopwatch (or watch with a second hand) and blindfold.

PARTICIPANTS: 4 children.

Participants compete with each other and the clock to see who can stuff the most toys in the bag within 20 seconds while blindfolded. Have the four participants come to the front of the room where the toys are spread out and the bag is located. You choose what order the children will play in. When each child's turn comes, count to three, and have everyone shout, "Stuff it!" Each child has 20 seconds to stuff the bag full of toys. Count the toys that are left out of the bag. The child who stuffs the most toys in the bag is the winner!

● **START**

PREP

Human Tic-Tac-Toe

PROPS: Masking tape, 12 pieces of construction paper and scissors.

With the masking tape, create a "tic-tac-toe" grid on the floor, at least six feet wide by six feet tall. Cut out six "X"s and six "O"s from the construction paper.

PLAYING

Divide all the children into two fairly even teams. One team will be "X"s and the other will be "O"s. Choose a captain for each team, and have them come to the front. Tape an X or an O on the front of the respective team captains.

Instruct the children that you are going to ask some review questions from the Bible Lesson that day, and each team will be given an opportunity to answer. If one team answers incorrectly, the other team will get the chance to answer. If neither team answers, repeat the procedure until one team answers correctly. Then ask the next question. The team captains will choose which kids on their teams will get to answer the review questions.

When a child answers the review question correctly, his captain will place a construction paper X or O (depending on the team) on his back with masking tape. The captain will then instruct the teammate with the X or O to take his place on the "tic-tac-toe" game board. The teammate gets to decide what position to stand in on the game board. The team that gets three in a row first wins!

YOU ARE HERE

● START

Musical Chairs

PROPS: Praise and Worship cassette, 5 chairs and cassette player.

PARTICIPANTS: 6 children.

Place five chairs in a circle. Have participants begin circling the chairs as music plays. Periodically stop the music. Children should scramble for a chair. The one who is left standing will be out of the game. Remove a chair as she leaves the game. The process is repeated until only one chair and two players remain. The last player to be seated in a chair when the music stops is the winner.

For a new twist, consider having the children play blindfolded.

Another alternative is to assign one chair (the last one to be removed) to be a bonus chair throughout the game. Every child who lands in that chair when the music stops gets a bonus or prize.

Make sure the children do not fight to sit in the chairs.

YOU ARE HERE

● **START**

PROPS: 6 balloons and 6 pieces of string, each 18 inches long. Tie the strings onto the balloons.

PARTICIPANTS: 3 boys and 3 girls.

Use loose end of string attached to balloons to tie around the left ankle of each participant. When the game begins, the players will try to pop one another's balloons by stomping on them. At the same time, each player must try to protect his own balloon. When a player's balloon is popped, he must immediately quit playing. The last person with an intact balloon is the winner.

Be sure the players understand they are supposed to pop one another's balloons and not their own.

START

PLAYING

The Great Snowball Fight

PROPS: 7 folding chairs and 100 pieces of wadded-up paper.

PARTICIPANTS: 3 boys and 3 girls.

Divide boys and girls into two teams. Divide the "snowballs" between each team as evenly as possible. Line up seven chairs in a straight line to form a divider. Have contestants kneel and toss their "snowballs" across the divider at the opposite team. After one minute, stop the game and count how many "snowballs" are on each side. The side with the fewest "snowballs" wins!

HINT

Be sure to have someone toss the "snowballs" back on the thrower's side if they are thrown out of bounds.

YOU ARE HERE

● **START**

PROPS: 18 chairs, 30 balloons and 2 pins.

PARTICIPANTS: 9 boys and 9 girls.

Set the chairs up one behind the other in two lines of nine each so that the children sitting on the chairs face the back of the person in front of them. Have the boys sit in one line and the girls in another. The captains should be at the end of each line. Each team has 15 balloons. When you say, "Go," have a helper hand the first balloon to the captain, who will lightly tap the balloon in the air to the person ahead of her. Each person continues to tap the balloon forward until it reaches the person in the front chair, who will grab the balloon and pop it with a pin. Each person in the line must tap the balloon. If the balloon escapes or misses a team member, a helper must grab it and bring it to the last person in the line who tapped it . Repeat with remaining balloons.

Players must stay in their seats. The balloons must be tapped in the air, not passed by hand.

Shoe Search

PARTICIPANTS: 2 teams (A and B) of 4 and captains.

Have all the participants take off their shoes and stack them in a big pile on the floor. Mix up the shoes. Next, have the players get in a circle around their shoes in alternating order—Team A player, Team B player, Team A player, Team B player and so on. The team captains should be standing 10 feet away on opposite sides of the circle.

When you say "Go," all the players find their own shoes, put them on, fasten them, then run to their team captain. The first team to get all their shoes on and to reach their captain is the winner.

● START

PLAYING

Cough-y Copy

PROPS: Box of tissues.

PARTICIPANTS: 3 boys and 3 girls.

Have the children stand shoulder-to-shoulder, facing the other children. Make a sickness sound, such as a single cough, that the first child must imitate. Then repeat the same cough and add a sneeze. The second child must imitate both sounds. Add another sickness sound and ask the third to imitate all three sounds. Continue adding sounds that the children must imitate. For example: fast cough, slow cough, tiny sneeze, loud sneeze, short sniffle, triple sneeze, double cough.

Whenever a child fails to repeat all of the sounds in the correct order, he is eliminated. The last child standing wins the box of tissues.

HINT

Make a list of the sounds and refer to it so you can be sure to repeat them in the correct order.

YOU ARE HERE

● **START** ------------------

Simon Peter Says

PARTICIPANTS: 3 boys and 3 girls.

Make a list of "fishing" commands and actions. The following are some suggestions: Make fish lips, swim like a fish, wiggle like a squid, crawl like a turtle, get into the boat, get down on your knees, pick up the net, cast your net into the sea, hold a fishing pole.

This is the familiar Simon Says game with added twists. The children are to follow your commands only when you have said "Simon Peter says...." Use "fishing" commands that illustrate John 21. Keep the kids up front as they are eliminated so you can thank them as a winning group for taking part.

Once the game is over, explain that when we obey the commands in the game we become winners. The closer we listen, the better are our chances of winning. More important than winning a game is the reward we have when we obey God. He gives us commands to help us in life, and when we choose to listen and obey, we will see the rewards.

● START

PLAYING

Hula Hoop Stuff

PROPS: 2 hula hoops.

PARTICIPANTS: 5 boys and 5 girls (to begin with).

Start with five boys and five girls. Group the members of each team as closely together as possible. Give each team a hula hoop to hold over their heads. Then have the players lower the hoops to their waists and raise them again. If a team can do this, they may add another teammate; then they lower and raise the hula hoop again. Continue playing until one team cannot get the hula hoop around their waists or until the hula hoop breaks. After this, the remaining team can keep adding players to see how far they can go.

HINT

Always have the same number of players.

YOU ARE HERE

21

● START

PLAYING

Silly Kings

PROPS: 2 chairs, 2 cans of Silly String and 2 rulers.

PARTICIPANTS: 2 boys and 2 girls.

One boy and one girl are the kings. Each sits on a "throne" (chair) facing the audience. The other two kids are crownmakers. They stand behind the kings with a can of Silly String. The challenge is to try to make the tallest pile of Silly String on the king's head. Give the crown-makers exactly one minute to work, then have your helpers measure the "crowns" with the rulers.

HINT

Have the helpers measure the crowns quickly because the Silly String might quickly fall flat or fall off.

YOU ARE HERE

● **START**

O pen up can of SpaghettiOs® and divide contents in half onto two plates.

**SpaghettiOs®
Eating Contest**

PROPS: 2 large napkins to tie around contestants' necks, 1 can of SpaghettiOs®, can opener and prize.

PARTICIPANTS: 2 children, time-keeper and judge.

Explain that the object of the game is to eat as much of the SpaghettiOs® as possible in the allotted time—the cleanest plate wins. Choose one of these two options: 1) use no hands, or 2) use hands (but no utensils). The time-keeper times the contest to last two minutes. Tie on napkins and say, "Go!" Be sure the kids in the audience can see the eaters during and after the event. The timekeeper shouts, "Stop!" at the two-minute mark. It should be a lot of fun! The judge selects the winner and awards the prize.

YOU
ARE
HERE

● START

Ice Cream Game

PROPS: 2 ice cream sandwiches (keep in freezer until game) and 2 paper plates.

PARTICIPANTS: 1 boy and 1 girl.

Place the ice cream sandwiches on the paper plates. Explain that the contest requires that the ice cream be swallowed. The contestant's mouth must be empty to win. The contest begins when you say "Go!" Check that the contestant's mouth is empty before declaring him or her a winner.

YOU ARE HERE

● **START**

PROPS: Bag of quality bubble gum.

PARTICIPANTS: Several boys and girls.

Give each child a piece of bubble gum. They may start chewing as soon as they receive the gum. It will take about three minutes before they have the gum ready to blow bubbles, so plan to have a song ready to sing during this time. "I Found a New Life" would be a good song to use. When the children are ready to compete, tell them they have one minute to blow the biggest bubble they can produce. Choose the three best bubble-blowers and have the others be seated. The top three will be given one minute to blow another bubble. Identify the one with the largest bubble and award this winner a prize (the rest of the bag of bubble gum).

Tell the children to keep the gum in their mouths when they sit down so it doesn't end up on the floor or underneath the chairs.

YOU ARE HERE

● START

PLAYING

Terrific Popcorn Toss

PROPS: 4 handfuls of popped popcorn, bags and stop watch (or watch with second-hand).

PARTICIPANTS: 4 children.

The four children will each choose a teammate from the remaining children in the group. At the front, have the teammates face each other, forming two parallel lines spaced about three feet apart. Give each of the first four kids a bag of popcorn.

Count to three, say "GO!" and allow 15 seconds for the original four participants to toss as much popcorn into their teammates' mouths as they can, one piece at a time. They cannot touch each other, and the teammate is not allowed to touch the popcorn or the bag.

At the end of 15 seconds, say "STOP!"

HINT

If you make enough popcorn, you may have them switch places with their teammates after the first 15 seconds and do it again! Be prepared for lots of laughs and a vacuum cleaning job afterward.

● **START**

Not So Mellow Marshmallow

PROPS: Table, 4 chairs, 2 bags of regular sized marshmallows; 4 paper plates and napkins and stopwatch (or watch with a second hand).

PARTICIPANTS: 4 children.

Set up table with four chairs at front of room.

Set the kids at the four places at the table. Give each child a paper plate and napkin. Place an equal, large number of marshmallows on each plate, and tell the children to wait until they are told to begin. At the count of three, give the children 15 seconds to eat as many marshmallows as they can. At the end of 15 seconds, tell them to stop. The child with the least number of marshmallows remaining wins! Let them eat any leftover marshmallows and clean up with the napkins. Depending on the size of your group, you may also want to have enough marshmallows to share with all the boys and girls.

If you have a tie, have a run-off contest with the two who tied. You'll need to have enough marshmallows for a run-off if necessary. You may need to let the participants wash up with soap and water following the marshmallow mess!

● **START**

PLAYING

Select four kids and allow them to choose four others to be their partners. Line them up, facing their partners, at the front of the room. Give the four kids each a banana. Instruct them not to do anything with the banana until you say, "Squish!" The contest is to see who can peel and feed a banana to her partner the fastest.

Tell the KIDS Church to count to three and shout, "Squish!" You and your workers watch to see who feeds the banana to her partner the fastest. She is the winner. Have the players put the banana peels and leftover banana squish in the trash can, and give them paper towels to clean themselves up.

Option: You may wish to give the winner some banana flavored candy or gum, or perhaps a gift certificate for a banana split at the local ice cream parlor.

HINT

If anyone who is chosen to be a partner does not like banana, do not force her to participate. Be sure to clean up all banana mess in the room and take out the trash when you are done. Banana has a very distinctive odor!

YOU ARE HERE

● START

PLAYING

Bubble-Gum Tape Race

PROPS: 2 rolls of bubble-gum tape, 2 stepladders (or chairs) and stopwatch. (Bubble-gum tape is a novelty dispenser of bubble gum available at variety stores.)

PARTICIPANTS: 1 boy, 1 girl and 2 adult helpers.

Set up the two ladders on stage. Have the helpers stand on the ladders, facing the audience. Have the two participants stand with their backs to the ladders so they are also facing the audience. The helpers each hold a bubble-gum tape dispenser. They will feed the bubble-gum tape to their players.

To begin, the helpers unroll the tape to reach to the players' mouths. When you say "Go," the kids begin to chew the gum and pull more bubble-gum tape into their mouths as fast as they can. They cannot use their hands.

The helpers unroll the gum, helping to "feed" their players. The time limit is 60 seconds. The winner is determined by measuring the remaining bubble-gum tape. Whichever player has the least remaining is the winner.

HINT

Instruct the helpers to use both hands and carefully dispense the gum. It can break easily, but with care it will unroll and not interrupt the game. A substitute for the gum tape game is dropping grapes or popcorn into the players' mouths and keeping count to determine a winner.

YOU ARE HERE

● **START**

PROPS: 4 large bags of peanuts; glass jar large enough to hold the peanuts (or bowl), table, 6 pieces of paper and 6 pencils.

PARTICIPANTS: 6 children.

Roasted Peanuts Mountain

Before the game, empty three bags of peanuts and count them. Make a note of the total. Put the peanuts into the jar, and place it on the table. Keep the fourth bag for a prize.

Instruct the participants to come to the table. Give them ten seconds to examine the jar of peanuts. They are not allowed to touch the jar. Tell them to write down their guess of the total number of peanuts in the jar. They are not allowed to tell anyone until everyone has written down his or her guess. When they are done, have them show you their written guesses. The one who comes the closest to the actual total number of peanuts wins the fourth (unopened) bag of peanuts. As a consolation prize, let the other five children reach into the jar to get a handful of peanuts.

START

PLAYING

Feed Me!

PROPS: 2 bowls of Jell-O® (or pudding) and 2 spoons. (Optional: 2 chairs.)

PARTICIPANTS: 4 children divided into 2 teams.

Have the first member of both teams sit cross-legged on the floor. Have them fold their hands behind their backs. The second team members must position themselves comfortably (suggest kneeling) behind the first, and insert their arms through their partners'. They will serve as the first players' "hands". Place a bowl of Jell-O® on the floor in front of player one, within reach of player two's hands. Lay a spoon beside the bowl. At the word "go," the player kneeling behind must pick up the spoon and feed his partner in front. The first to empty the bowl wins!

YOU ARE HERE

● **START**

PLAYING

Popcorn Frenzy

PROPS: 7 small bags of popcorn and stopwatch (or watch with second hand).

PARTICIPANTS: 6 children.

The six participants will choose six partners from the group. Have all 12 come to the front of the room and form two parallel lines, with participants and partners facing each other. Tell them that when you count to three, the children who were chosen to be partners will have 15 seconds to stuff as much popcorn as they can into the mouths of their participant teammates. Hand the bags of popcorn to the chosen partners and count to three. At 15 seconds, tell them to stop. The participant whose partner's bag contains the least amount of popcorn is declared the winner! Give the winner the seventh bag of popcorn.

START

Spread the Bread

PROPS: 1 loaf of soft, white bread, 2 jars of peanut butter, 6 butter knives, 6 paper plates, napkins or paper towels, large table with 6 chairs set up in front of everyone and stopwatch (or watch with second hand).

PARTICIPANTS: 6 children.

Have kids take a seat in the chairs at the table. Give them each a paper plate, a knife and a napkin. Instruct them that once they begin, they have 30 seconds to spread peanut butter on one side of their piece of bread. The person who spreads the peanut butter on one side of her piece without tearing it wins the contest! Hand each participant a piece of bread and open the peanut butter jars. Remind them that they will have to share the peanut butter jars. Count to three, and have everyone shout, "Spread the bread!" After 30 seconds, tell them to stop. Examine the pieces of bread. The one who did the best spreading job is the winner! Let the players eat their sandwiches. Have them clean up with the napkins.

You may have a player who doesn't like peanut butter. Have an alternative prize to give her.

START

Soda Pop Shake Up

PROPS: Six-pack of soda pop, 6 hand towels, soapy water and sponge for clean-up.

PARTICIPANTS: 6 children.

Have participants come to the front of the room. Give each an unopened soda pop can. Tell them that the object is to shake up the soda pop, place their mouths over the opening, pop off the top, and try to get as much spraying soda pop into their mouths as possible! Have them shake up their cans, and then, when you think that the soda is foamy enough, have them put their mouths over the opening. You count down from five to one, and shout "Blast off!" as they open the tops to the cans. When they have finished, give each one a hand towel to wipe up the mess. If they have any soda pop left in their cans, let them drink it. Have one of your workers wipe up any mess on the walls, floors, etc. with the soapy water and sponge.

Choose only one flavor/type of soda pop for all the participants. This avoids arguments over which flavor they want or don't want. If a participant does not like the flavor you have, have an alternate contestant for him. Also, be aware that it is possible that a child may get soda pop into the nose or eyes. This is only a temporary discomfort and will not do any real harm.

YOU ARE HERE

● **START**

Place the bowls and string on the table in front of everyone, with the chairs around the table. Fill the bowls with Cheerios® and set a bowl in front of each place at the table.

Let each participant choose four "Cheerios® Cheerleaders" from the rest of the children. The object is to see which player can thread the most Cheerios® on the string in 60 seconds. Have the four players sit in the chairs at the table. Tell the "Cheerios® Cheerleaders" to stand behind their players. Give each of the players a string. Explain the object of the game, and then have them each tie a Cheerios® onto one end of their string. (This will keep the other Cheerios® on the string when they are threading them during the game.) Then say, "Let's make Cheerios® Chains!" and count down from five to zero. Time them for 60 seconds and then tell them to stop. You and a worker count the number of Cheerios® each player has threaded onto her string. The one with the most wins! Let the players keep or eat her Cheerios® Chains. Give the winner the box of Cheerios® with any leftover cereal.

● START

PLAYING

L et the first player run to the fruit bowl and grab a piece of fruit. He should chew it, swallow it, run back to his partner, tag his hand and let the partner run to the fruit bowl. Continue the relay until one team finishes eating all the fruit in the bowl.

HINT

This can be messy. Ask the participants to wear towels over their clothes. Have some wet washcloths ready for their hands when the game is over.

Pig-Out Relay

PROPS: 2 bowls with cubed fruit (watermelon, if in season), wet washcloths and towels.

PARTICIPANTS: 2 boys and 2 girls.

YOU ARE HERE

START

Super Sloppy Egg Drop

PROPS: 10 eggs, 2 plastic cups and plastic trash bags.

PARTICIPANTS: 2 boys and 2 girls (wearing slacks).

Cover the floor with the plastic bags so that broken eggs will not mess up the floor. Have one boy and one girl lie on their backs with their feet facing the audience. Cover their clothes and hair with the other plastic bags. Have them hold cups over their mouths. The other two players will stand or kneel on a chair over their teammates. When you say "Go," the two on the chairs will crack open their eggs and attempt to drop the contents of the egg into the cup. After five tries for each team, the game is over. Whichever has the most egg inside the cup wins.

Cover only the child's hair and not her face with the plastic bags. After the game is over, make sure the players do not track egg off the plastic. It's funny to see who has the most egg on her face! You may wish to have the kids on the floor wear goggles or snorkel masks!

● **START**

Fill the pitchers with juice. Place them side-by-side on a table. Have the players on each team stand behind a line at least 10 feet from the pitchers. Each player has a straw. When you say "Go," the first boy and girl run to their respective pitchers of juice and begin drinking from them with their straws. After several seconds, blow your whistle. They must instantly stop drinking, run to their second teammates, tag them and line up behind their third teammates.

Repeat this with the second and third players. Repeat for one more round so that each player drinks twice.

It's fun to vary the amount of time you let the kids drink. One turn might be quite long, the next one very short. Play for about two minutes. The team which drinks the most (or finishes its pitcher first) is the winner.

Be sure everyone in the audience can see the pitchers.

● **START**

PLAYING

Hangin' Hot Dogs

PROPS: 4 cooked hot dogs, 4 pieces of string and pole.

PARTICIPANTS: 2 boys and 2 girls.

Tie one end of each piece of string to one end of a hot dog. Tie the other ends of the string to the pole at evenly spaced intervals. Secure pole in a horizontal position or have helpers hold it in place.

Make sure that the hot dogs hang directly in front of kids' mouths. When you say "Go," have the kids eat their hot dogs as fast as they can. The first one finished wins.

The kids must have their hands behind their backs as they eat their hot dogs. It's helpful to have a keyboard player playing up-tempo, game-show type tunes.

HINT

Do not tie the hot dogs in the middle! Tie them close to one end. Instruct the players to start at the bottom and eat until they finish. Warn them that they can't pull the hot dog off the string or cause it to fall off. If they do, they'll be disqualified. Also remind them that they have to swallow the whole hot dog to be finished.

YOU ARE HERE

● **START**

Soda Slurp

PROPS: 2 sodas in clear bottles (or glasses) and 2 straws.

PARTICIPANTS: 1 boy and 1 girl.

Place the two sodas on the table. Put the straws in them. With their hands behind their backs, the players must drink the sodas. They must use only the straws and cannot use their hands in any way. The first player with every drop gone is the winner.

Select older children and allow them to pass if they are not comfortable with playing.

● **START**

PLAYING

Chewy Relay

PROPS: 2 jars of peanut butter, 2 knives and loaf of bread.

PARTICIPANTS: 2 boys and 2 girls.

Place on the table the open jars of peanut butter, knives and half a loaf of bread for each team. Have a helper at the table to supervise.

When you say "Go," the first boy and girl run from one side of the stage to the table and take a piece of bread, put some peanut butter on it, fold it in half and take a bite, then chew and chew and chew and swallow. The helper determines a fair bite and the chew and swallow process (no baby bites).

As the helper gives the signal, the players run back to tag their partners for the next sandwich run. The team members alternate turns, piling up the peanut butter sandwiches from which they've taken a bite. Suggested time limit is two minutes.

If the game is close, blow the whistle and end the game at a time when there is a clear winner. If both teams are in the middle of chewing, give the game a few more seconds until it's obvious who is clearly ahead. Count discarded sandwiches to determine the winning team.

START

PLAYING

Interceding Seedless Grapes

PROPS: Pair of new tube socks, scissors and bowl of seedless grapes.

PARTICIPANTS: 2 teams of 2 children each and 2 adult helpers to count.

Cut two small holes in the toes of the socks. Use two adult helpers as counters and be sure the players are set up so the audience can see them.

The interceders (captains) place the socks on their hands. Their index and middle fingers should stick out of the holes. They can only use these two fingers to pick up the grapes, one at a time.

Interceders start feeding their partners on the "Go!" command. The team that eats the most grapes in one minute is the winner.

● START

PLAYING

PROPS: 2 liters of soda, small paper cups and stopwatch.

PARTICIPANTS: 1 boy, 1 girl and kids seated in front row.

hen you say "Go," each child fills one paper cup halfway (not full) with soda. The boy serves his cup to one of the boys seated in the front row, and the girl does the same for her side. Both kids drink the soda and give the cups back to their servers.

The servers return to the soda table, get a clean paper cup, fill it halfway and race to serve another kid. Repeat, serving as many cups of soda as possible to teammates. Suggested time limit is two minutes. The team with the most used cups is the winner.

HINT

Kids are to fill cups halfway so spills are minimal. Helpers can collect used cups for the official count.

YOU ARE HERE

● **START**

Line up participants and give each a strand of licorice. Have them put the tip of their licorice sticks into their mouths and put their hands behind their backs.

When you say "Go," they need to chew the licorice and draw it into their mouths as fast as possible without using their hands. The winner is the first one with the entire piece in his mouth.

Avoid using young children and make sure all participants are willing to participate. Have extra pieces of licorice on hand, in case a participant drops his strand or a restart is needed.

● **START**

Whistling Dixie

PROPS: 6 saltine crackers.

PARTICIPANTS: 3 boys and 3 girls.

G ive each child a cracker. When you say "Go," the kids will chew their crackers, swallow them and then try to whistle. The team with all three players whistling first wins. Spitting out the cracker eliminates the entire team.

● START

Fruit Loopin' Pizza

PROPS: Fruit Loops® cereal, 4 small slivers of pizza, 2 plates and table.

PARTICIPANTS: 1 boy and 1 girl.

Place the plates on the table. Put two small pieces of pizza on each plate. Pour cereal over the pizza so the pieces are completely covered.

Have the participants stand at the starting line, facing the audience. The table should be about 25 feet away. Let the players know that they may not use their hands. When you say "Go," they run to the table. Using only their mouths, they eat through the Fruit Loops® until they can get one piece of pizza in their mouths. Holding the pizza with their mouths, they run back to the starting line. They chew the pizza while facing the audience. They repeat the process with the second piece of pizza. The first one to finish both pieces is the winner.

Keep the pizza pieces small. Consider using plastic trash bags to cover the children's clothes.

START

PLAYING

PROPS: 2 hard boiled eggs (still in the shells) and 2 plastic pig noses.

PARTICIPANTS: 1 boy and 1 girl.

Mark a finish line at center stage and two starting lines at opposite ends, each about 20 feet from the finish line. Players put on the plastic noses and get down on their hands and knees. The egg is placed on the starting line. Using only their snouts, players push the egg toward the finish line. The first to cross the finish line is the winner.

HINT

Out-of-bounds lines may be needed to guide the participants.

YOU ARE HERE

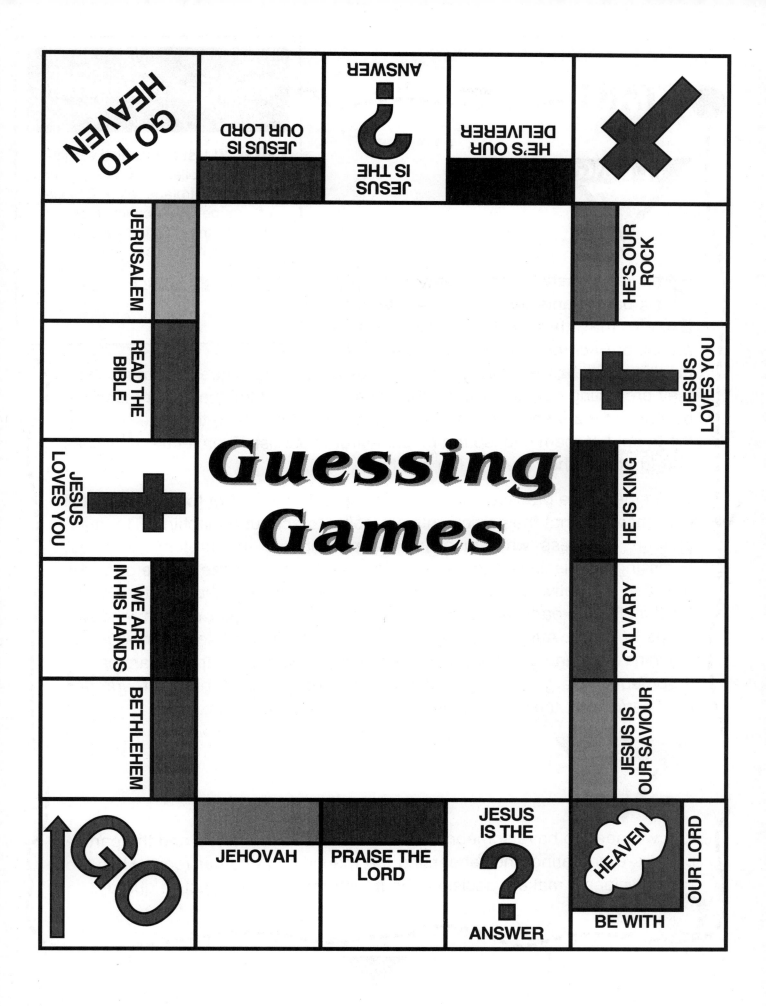

START

Maniac Machine

PROPS: List of machines (such as automobile, truck, boat, pinball machine, airplane, etc.), 6 pieces of wrapped hard candy, 6 small candy bars and stopwatch (or watch with a second hand).

PARTICIPANTS: 6 children.

PLAYING

This is a "charade" type game. Have the six participants go into a separate area. Explain that they will be acting out a machine. Each of them will be a part of the machine and the rest of the children will be attempting to guess what machine they are acting out. Show them the candy bars, and tell them that these will be their prizes if someone is able to guess what machine they are pretending to be. Let them choose the machine from your list. Then let them discuss and "practice" their parts of the machine.

When they have practiced a little, bring them to the front of the room and tell the other kids that the participants are going to act out a machine. The audience is to guess what machine the participants are pretending to be. Guessing time is limited to one minute, and there is a prize for the one who guesses correctly. Count to three and have everyone shout out, "Maniac Machine!" The participants form their machine, and you call on whoever wants to guess. After one minute, if no one has guessed, tell them what the machine was, and give the participants a small piece of wrapped hard candy. If someone has guessed the machine, she gets a small piece of wrapped hard candy and the participants each get a small candy bar.

HINT

You will need to have someone lead KIDS Church while you and the participants are preparing and rehearsing the machine in another room. Help the participants make a decision about the machine and practice quickly.

YOU ARE HERE

● **START**

The Winning Envelope

PROPS: 8 large envelopes, slips of paper and prize (or winner's certificate).

PARTICIPANTS: 2 teams with 4 members on each.

Mark the front of the envelopes with numbers 1 through 8. Write "Sorry" on seven slips of paper and insert in envelopes. Write "Winner" on one slip and put it in the eighth envelope. You may want to mount the envelopes on a portable chalkboard or large poster.

Determine which team will go first and ask them a Bible Lesson review question. Let the team members work together, and have an assigned leader give you their answer. A correct answer allows them the chance to choose an envelope. Allow a few moments for the teammates to yell out their suggestions for the envelope choice. The teams alternate turns until the winning envelope is found.

Award the winning team a prize.

● **START**

Gum Ball Guessers

PROPS: Clear gum-ball machine (or clear jar) filled with gum balls and envelope.

PARTICIPANTS: All boys and girls in the audience.

Count the gum balls as you place them in the machine. Write the total on a piece of paper and place it inside a sealed envelope. Also record the total so it is available to you as you begin the game.

Have kids guess how many gum balls are in the machine. Starting with the girls, accept answers alternately from the girls' and boys' sides. Have a helper carry the gum-ball machine around so the children can see it as they guess.

As each guess is made, tell the kids whether the actual number is higher or lower. The helper walks between the two teams as they continue to guess. If a girl guesses correctly, divide the gum among the girls. If a boy guesses correctly, divide the gum among the boys.

YOU ARE HERE

● START

The object is to guess the praise tunes as the instrumental is played. Prepare at least eight selections of music for the game. Make sure they are songs that the children will be able to recognize.

Each team lines up facing the audience. They may only guess or speak when they have been called on.

Participants raise their hands to make guesses. The correct answer is rewarded with a prize. Participants must sit down if their guesses are wrong. However, consider awarding a consolation prize.

To make the game more challenging and instructional, ask the child who correctly names the tune to state whether it is a praise song (a song about the Lord or His attributes) or a worship song (a song that is sung to the Lord).

Name That Tune

PROPS: Familiar Praise and Worship cassette (instrumental only) and candy (or small prizes). Note: You can use a musician if you prefer.

PARTICIPANTS: 2 teams of 6 children.

● **START**

PLAYING

Character Sketch

PROPS: List of 5 Bible characters you have studied within the last 2 months.

PARTICIPANTS: 5 boys and 5 girls.

Pick three Bible characters with which the children will be familiar. One member of each team steps forward to represent the rest. Each takes a turn asking any yes or no question to help them figure out the character, alternating back and forth between teams. The first to correctly guess the character, scores one point for his team. (A guess must be taken instead of a question.) If he guesses incorrectly, the point automatically goes to the opposite side. Let each child on the two sides have one chance to play. The team to score the most points wins.

YOU
ARE
HERE

● **START**

PLAYING

Directions In the Dark

PROPS: Blindfold, funny hat, bag of popcorn, small bowl and stopwatch.

PARTICIPANTS: 1 boy and 1 girl.

Your players will need to rely on you for their directions. Let them compete one at a time against the clock. Blindfold the first player, then place the props. Keep them at close range, but spaced apart. Tell the children how to find the items and what to do with them. For example: "The bag of popcorn is two big steps to your left; pick it up. Now find the bowl—it's right behind you. Fill it with popcorn. Now go four steps to your right, pick up the hat and put it on." Have your second contestant try to beat the time of the first player.

HINT

Experiment with the various tasks in advance to be sure they will work well for your group.

YOU ARE HERE

●START

Have the players get inside the playpen and cover their eyes. A worker then buries a dry sponge in the balls. The kids must search through with their hands. The one to find the object wins.

Encourage everyone to cheer with enthusiasm.

Playpen Mania

PROPS: Large fenced-in area to create a playpen look, enough small balls (or balloons) to cover the floor, creating 2 or more layers, and 1 dry sponge (or other detectable object).

PARTICIPANTS: 1 boy and 1 girl.

YOU ARE HERE

● **START**

PROPS: List of things that children would have with them when they come to church—comb, money, Bible, pencil, red shoe, picture of someone, blue coat, etc.

PARTICIPANTS: You, 2 adult workers and all of the children.

Divide your kids into two teams, using your adult workers as leaders. Call out items from your list. Both workers will run into the audience and try to find team members who have the items. The first worker to bring all the items to the stage and put them in your hands is the winner.

Example: You call out "black shoe, blue barrette, red comb." Both adult workers run out and try to find someone wearing a black shoe, then someone wearing a blue barrette and someone who has a red comb. The children who have the items give them to the worker, who brings them all to you and puts them in your hands. Be sure that your workers are able to run around with ease because this game can be very tiring for them.

Be sure to explain to the children that they must remain in their seats. If they try to run up to the stage and hand you the article themselves, someone might get hurt.

● **START**

PROPS: 2 canvas mail bags (filled with envelopes, newspaper, letters and paper), 2 envelopes and marker.

PARTICIPANTS: 2 children.

Write the first participant's name on one of the envelopes. Hide it in his or her mailbag. Do the same with the other. When you say "Go," the kids are to empty their mailbags, find the letters with their names on them, put all the other paper back in their bags, and hand you their envelopes. The first one to do that wins.

Use large, bold print on the kids' envelopes so they can easily recognize their envelopes.

● **START**

PLAYING

PROPS: 2 clothes hangers, 10 clothespins, 2 large trash cans filled with paper trash and 10 construction-paper fish.

PARTICIPANTS: 2 boys and 2 girls.

Write one letter on each fish, spelling out "Jesus" twice. Each team will have five fish. Hide the fish sets in the trash cans. When you say, "Go!" the players will run to their trash cans and find their fish. Once a team finds all five fish, the players must pin them on the hanger using the clothespins. Each team must hang the fish in the correct order to read "Jesus." The first team to get the fish in order wins.

HINT

Be sure the players face the audience when playing.

YOU ARE HERE

START

PLAYING

Seed Spit

PROPS: 2 plates full of watermelon seeds and 2 bowls (or snack buckets).

PARTICIPANTS: 1 girl and 1 boy.

Have a worker hold the plate full of seeds in front of the audience. On "Go," each player grabs a seed with her mouth, runs to the other end of the room and spits the seed into a bowl (one bowl for each kid). Then they must run back and grab another seed and do the same. The one to fill the bowl with the most seeds in two minutes wins.

● START

Of all the games, the obstacle course is the most versatile. Basically, you need five or six things for the kids to do. It's good to have all the actions related, thereby allowing the game to have a theme.

Time the first participant as he runs the obstacle course. Then time the second participant. Whoever runs the course the fastest wins.

Get Ready for School!

1. Throw ball at alarm clock.

2. Put on jogging suit (over clothing!).

3. Eat pancake.

4. Brush teeth.

5. Run out door.

K.P. Duty!

1. Sweep up paper wads with broom.

2. Hang clothes on line.

3. Dry dishes.

4. Take out bag of trash.

5. Make bed.

Have a dry run with some kids beforehand so you can iron out any problems before you use it with your kids.

The Obstacle Course

Props: Here are two lists of themed props. Use your imagination to create your own obstacle course! List 1: Ball, alarm clock, jogging suit, pancake, toothbrush and doorway. List 2: Broom, paper wads, clothes, clothesline, clothespins, dishes, dish towel, bag of trash, table ("bed") and sheet.

Participants: 2 or more children.

YOU ARE HERE

● **START** - - - - - - - - - - - - - -

Lemon Shaker

PROPS: 2 lemon wedges, 2 tablespoons of sugar and 2 cups of water.

PARTICIPANTS: 2 children.

At one end of the room have the two players. At the other end have all of the props. When the game starts, both players run to the prop table and eat a lemon wedge. When they finish, they run back to the starting point. Then they race back to the table and eat their spoonful of sugar, run back to the starting point and back to the prop table. There they will drink the cup of water. The last part of the game is to mix the lemonade ingredients up in their stomach, so when they finish drinking the water, they need to jump up and down ten times. The first person to do this wins.

Explain to the kids and participants how to run the lemonade race. Show them by walking them through it, then play the game.

Please practice the game so it goes quickly and smoothly.

● START

The sack race has been around for so long it needs no explanation. However, for those of you who may suffer from GDD (Game Deficit Disorder)...what you do is have each child step into the sack, hold onto the edges and hop from one end of the room to the other. The first one to cross the finish line wins. As a variation, require the children to recite a word from a memory verse with every hop.

Be sure the length of the course is long enough to require about one minute to complete. The two participants need to be about the same size.

Sack Race

PROPS: 2 potato sacks (burlap bags or plastic bags).

PARTICIPANTS: 2 or more children.

YOU ARE HERE

● **START** - - - - - - - - - - - - - - - - -

Scripture Relay

PROPS: 2 chalkboards (or easels with paper), 2 pieces of chalk (or markers or appropriate writing instruments).

PARTICIPANTS: 2 teams of mixed boys and girls (number depends on Scripture verse chosen).

Select a verse from the Bible and read it aloud several times to the two teams (such as John 3:16). At the word "GO," the first player on each team runs to the chalkboard and writes clearly the first word of the Scripture verse. Then they must run back and hand the chalk to the second member on the team. The second member runs to the board and writes the second word of the verse, and so on. The first team to complete the verse correctly wins. Team members may help their teammates remember which word comes next.

YOU
ARE
HERE

● **START**

PROPS: 2 pairs of extra-large long underwear, 50 small inflated balloons in a bag and pin (or dart).

PARTICIPANTS: 2 boys and 2 girls.

Have one boy and one girl put on long underwear over their regular clothes. They are designated as the "turkeys." Place the bag of balloons about 20 feet from the "turkeys." The other participants are the "stuffers."

When you say "Go," the "stuffers" run to the bag of balloons, take one, run back and stuff it in the long underwear of their "turkey." They will have one minute to stuff as many balloons as possible into the long underwear.

Be sure that the children stuffing the balloons in the long underwear distribute the balloons all around the "turkey." Helpers can help by pointing to areas that need to be stuffed and that can handle more balloons.

After the minute is up, count the number of balloons for each team, popping them one by one with a pin as you count. The team with the most balloons stuffed is the winner.

Be sure that the girl chosen to be the "turkey" is wearing slacks.

YOU ARE HERE

● **START**

PREP

Shootin' the Breeze Relay Race

PROPS: 2 styrofoam cups, roll of string, scissors, masking tape and 4 chairs.

PARTICIPANTS: 6 boys or girls.

Punch a small hole in the bottom of both cups. Cut 2 pieces of string at least 15 feet long (or as long as the width of your room will allow). Place chairs at the front of the room, two on one side and two on the other side, at least 15 feet apart. They should also be about six feet from one another on each side of the room. Take the string and tape one end of each string to the backs of one set of chairs on one side of the room. Then, thread one cup onto each string through the hole in the bottom. Take the free end of the string to the other side of the room and tape it to the back of the chair that is directly opposite the one to which it is already attached. Adjust both strings until they are fairly taut. You should have two parallel strings across the front of your room with a styrofoam cup on each string. Slide both cups to the chair backs on one side of the room. Have workers sit in chairs to steady them.

PLAYING

The six participants will each choose another kid. Divide them into two teams. In relay race fashion, send Team 1 to opposite chairs directly across the room from one another, three kids to each chair. Do the same with Team 2. Instruct both teams that the object of the game is for each person on their team, one at a time, to blow the cup on the string across the room to their teammates on the other side, and then their teammates are to blow the cup back to the side where they began. They are to continue to do this until the last person on their team has blown the cup across. The team which accomplishes this first wins. They are not to use their hands or touch the cup in any way. When they are not blowing the cup, they need to stay in line next to the chair for their team. Have the whole audience shout, "On your mark, Get set, GO!" Award treats to the winning team.

● START

The Great Balloon Run

PROPS: 10 inflated balloons, 2 baskets and masking tape. (Note: Make sure that the balloons are blown up all the way or they will not pop.)

PARTICIPANTS: 1 boy and 1 girl.

Set the two baskets at the back of the auditorium and place five balloons in each basket. A starting point for a relay race should be determined and marked with tape.

Have both children stand on the taped starting line. Say "Go!" Children will run to the baskets at the back of the room and grab one balloon each. They will return to the starting line and sit on the balloon until it pops. This process will continue for all five balloons. The first child to pop all five wins.

Be sure the girl who participates is not wearing a dress.

Note: You may wish to do this game as a relay race by allowing each participant to choose four teammates.

YOU ARE HERE

● **START**

PLAYING

PARTICIPANTS: 2 teams, one consisting of 4 boys and the other consisting of 4 girls.

Have both teams sit on the floor. Have the four boys link arms back to back and the four girls do the same. Now have all four try to stand up. The team that stands up first wins. You may want to have them stand up then race across a finish line at the other side of the room.

HINT

Players should be approximately the same size.

YOU ARE HERE

● **START**

When you say "Go," have the children blow up their balloons. Release the balloons and they will sail through the air. The participants must then go to where their balloons land, stop and blow them up again and repeat the whole process until one of the balloons crosses the goal line, which should be set about 25 feet away.

Be sure the balloons are easy to blow up.

Hot Air Balloon Race

PROPS: 2 balloons.

PARTICIPANTS: 1 boy and 1 girl.

● **START**

PLAYING

Basketball Relay

PROPS: 2 basketballs.

PARTICIPANTS: 2 girls and 2 boys.

Divide the boys and girls into two teams of two. Have teammates stand back to back with the basketball suspended between them. The ball should be placed in the small of the players' backs. Each team must carry the ball to the goal line and back to where they started. The first team to do that wins. If the team drops the ball, they must begin again.

HINT

The participants need to be about the same size. They must keep their arms folded in front of them. They are not allowed to use their elbows to hold the ball in their backs.

YOU ARE HERE

● **START**

Toilet Paper Roll

PROPS: 2 rolls of toilet paper, 2 pencils and 2 chairs.

PARTICIPANTS: 2 boys and 2 girls.

Place each pencil in one of the cardboard rolls. One boy and one girl will stand on a chair and hold the ends of a pencil (so the paper will unroll easily). The other two kids will stand below their partners and pull the toilet paper off the roll. The team that pulls all the paper off first wins.

Option: For a variation, have one member of each team wrap her partner like a mummy, running around and around her with the toilet paper. The first to use up the whole roll wins. Colored crepe paper also works well.

● **START** - - - - - - - - - - - - - - - - -

House Dressing

PROPS: 2 pairs of very large pants, 2 very large dresses, 2 old coats and 2 hats.

PARTICIPANTS: 1 boy and 1 girl.

Have the players stand next to you at one end of the stage. Lay the two sets of clothes at the opposite end. On your signal, each child runs to the other end of the stage and puts on the pair of pants. Then they must run back to you at the starting line, tag your hand and run back to the clothes to put on the dresses. They tag you again, then run back to put on the coats. Finally, they put on the hats. The first child to finish getting dressed is the winner.

YOU ARE HERE

Be sure the old clothes are very large so the kids can get them on easily. Have the kids remove their shoes so they can get the pants on quickly.

● **START**

Balloon Pass

PROPS: 2 balloons.

PARTICIPANTS: 7 boys and 7 girls.

Each team gets in a single-file line. Give the first boy and girl a balloon. At your signal, the first kids will pass the balloons over their heads to the persons behind them, who pass it between their legs to the next persons, who pass it over their heads to the next persons, and so on. When the last kids in line get the balloon, they run to the front of the line and start the passing again. The game continues until the kids who were originally first in line make it to the back of the line, receive the balloon, and run back to the front of the line.

Have helpers watch carefully to make sure the kids pass the balloon in the right way (over and under, over and under), but make sure the helpers don't block the audience's view.

● START - - - - - - - - - - - - - - - - - -

Stepping Stones

PROPS: 4 sheets of construction paper.

PARTICIPANTS: 1 boy and 1 girl.

Set up an obstacle course by arranging chairs, tables, props, etc.

Give each child two pieces of construction paper to use as stepping stones. The object of the game is for the kids to go through a small obstacle course that you have set up without letting their feet touch the floor. They have to move their papers before they take the next step. The first one to complete the course without stepping off the papers wins.

HINT

If you play the game on a slick floor, the kids may try to move their papers by shuffling their feet. Do not allow this.

● **START**

Four-Legged Race

PROPS: 6 pieces of rope (or twine) and stopwatch.

PARTICIPANTS: 3 boys and 3 girls.

Have the three teammates stand shoulder to shoulder. Take the rope and tie each leg of the person in the middle to both partner's legs.

The object of the game is to run to a designated spot at the opposite end of the room and back as quickly as possible. The difficulty comes in coordinating the players motions as they run the race with their legs tied together.

YOU ARE HERE

Be sure the rope is not tied too tightly around the children's legs.

If the game area is too small, have the teams run separately. (You will need a stopwatch to time each team.)

● **START**

PLAYING

Kid Glove Relay

PROPS: 2 pairs of gloves, 2 shirts (with buttons), 2 bananas and pair of shoes with laces.

PARTICIPANTS: 1 boy and 1 girl.

The children put on a pair of gloves and try to complete the required tasks at the game stations. There is one task at each of three stations. Upon hearing "Go," they must do the following:

Station One—Put on a shirt and button three buttons.

Station Two—Peel a banana and eat it.

Station Three—Tie a shoe lace.

The first contestant to complete the tasks is the winner.

This game can be difficult if the gloves are too thick. Have a trial run before the service. If the trial run takes more than a couple of minutes, you may need to simplify the tasks.

● **START**

D ivide the soda cans equally between the boys and girls. Scatter the boys' soda cans on one side of the room and the girls' on the other. Give each team one empty trash bag.

Establish a time limit of two minutes. When you say "Go," each team runs to pick up their empty soda cans. They are allowed to work as a team however they want. They must gather all their empties and put them in the bag.

Next, they run to the front and build a tower by stacking the cans on the table. The first team to stack six cans is the winner.

YOU ARE HERE

Consider your room size as you set the time limit for the game.

Recycle Towers

PROPS: Empty soda cans (24-36), 2 trash bags and table.

PARTICIPANTS: 2 boys and 2 girls.

● **START**

PLAYING

PROPS: 12 balloons, large box, 2 chairs, 12 small slips of colored paper, marker and stopwatch.

PARTICIPANTS: 1 boy, 1 girl and 2 adult helpers.

Roll the small slips of paper and place them in balloons, then inflate and tie the balloons. Place the balloons in a large open box and put it in the game area.

Have the participants sitting in the chairs, facing the audience. When you say "Go," they run to the box, take one balloon apiece, return to their chairs and sit on the balloons until they pop.

They must find the slip of paper in each balloon and give it to their helper. Then they race to take another balloon and repeat the process until all balloons are gone or 60 seconds have elapsed.

The helpers then tally the slips to determine who has the most

● START

PLAYING

YOU ARE HERE

Tug of War

PROPS: Hefty rope (approximately 10-25 feet long) and scarf.

PARTICIPANTS: 3 boys and 3 girls (the two sides need to be about the same size) and some adult workers.

Have three participants on one side of the rope and the other three on the other side. At the count of three, have them start pulling. You stand in the middle, watching to see who will pull the other side past you.

Whichever team pulls the other team past you first wins the game. Give them each a prize. For a variation, have just one girl and one boy play. Since boys always seem confident they can beat girls at this game, it's always fun to "stack the deck" by adding more girls to the girls' side and watch them pull the guys over.

HINT

Be sure you have a spotter or some adult worker behind each team, in case one team decides to let go of the end of the rope at the end of the game. This game actually turns into an object lesson on faithfulness. Often the team that starts out strong in the beginning loses to the team that can "endure" to the end. God doesn't want good starters in His army. He wants good finishers!

● **START**

PROPS: 2 transparencies of the same picture with slight alterations in one, 2 pencils, 2 pieces of paper and stopwatch.

Divide kids into a boys' team and a girls' team. Teams will try to find differences between the two pictures. Give each team captain a piece of paper and pencil to record their answers.

Project the transparencies. Explain to the kids that these pictures look the same at first glance, but as they look closer, they will discover big differences. Ask them to find and list as many as they can as fast as they can. Encourage them to work quietly so they don't give away their answers. Team members should whisper their answers for the captains to record.

Allow the teams 60 to 90 seconds to record their answers. Take the lists and check them aloud as you verify the answers. Announce the winners.

● START -

PROPS: Masking tape.

PARTICIPANTS: 3 children.

PREP

Mark off three squares with the masking tape.

PLAYING

YOU ARE HERE

Assign each child to one square. When you say "Go!" the kids begin to hop up and down on one foot, holding the other off the ground. They may switch feet at any time but must always keep one in the air and remain within the boundaries of their square. Whoever lasts the longest wins.

For a variation in the game, time them for two minutes. Whoever hops the most number of times, wins. You will need a separate worker to observe each child and count carefully.

● **START**

Can Stacking

PROPS: 1 table and 10 to12 empty soda cans (If the kids are smaller, use 10 empty soda cans; if the kids are larger, use 12 empty soda cans.)

PARTICIPANTS: 2 boys and 2 girls. Split the kids into two teams.

Cans are divided evenly between the two teams. When you say "Go!" the children have to stack the cans one on top of the other and make a tower. If the cans fall over, a worker picks them up and puts them back on the table. The winner of the game is the team that is first to make all of their cans stand up without holding them. The cans have to be standing up unassisted.

The soda cans should be empty so if they fall they won't burst open.

● **START** - - - - - - - - - - - - - - - - - - -

PROPS: Overhead projector, stopwatch, transparency of a Scripture verse that has been cut up and prize.

PARTICIPANTS: 1 boy, 1 girl and stopwatch operator.

Review the Scripture verse so everyone in the audience knows it. Turn off the projector and scramble the transparency. Explain to the audience that the top and bottom of the projector image are reversed.

Have one of the participants come to the overhead projector. When you say "Go!" he is to unscramble the verse so it reads correctly and right-side up. Turn on the projector and say "Go!" The stopwatch operator is to keep time. Follow the same procedure with the other participant. The one who correctly unscrambles the verse in the shortest time wins. Present a prize.

● **START**

PLAYING

PROPS: Bag of dried peas, 8 butter knives, stopwatch and can of split pea soup.

PARTICIPANTS: 2 boys and 2 girls.

YOU ARE HERE

Have four contestants each choose another person to play this game. When they have all come to the front of the room, hand each one a butter knife. They have 20 seconds to get as many peas as they can to stay on their butter knives. Give them each a handful of peas, and count down. Count to three and say, "Pea Party Time." When the 20 seconds are up, have the remaining kids shout "Pea Party Time!" You and your workers must count the peas to determine who has the most peas on her butter knife. The winner gets the "gag" prize— the can of split pea soup!

START

YOU ARE HERE

BIBLE BASEBALL

PROPS: Prizes, bat and soft Nerf®-style ball.

All the children are involved in this unusual game of "baseball." Take the bat and hit the ball to one side of the room. If a child catches the "baseball" from a seated position, have him come to the stage area with you.

There is no limit to the number of people allowed on stage from each team. There are three ways a team can make an out:

1. If the ball hits the ground before it is caught—it's an out.

2. If the child stands up to catch the ball—it's an out.

3. If there is any fighting—it's an out.

After three outs, go to the opposite side of the room. The side with the most kids up front wins.

To stretch the game out longer, prepare in advance several questions from the previous week's Bible Lesson. Ask the winning group to line up facing the audience. Have a leader read the the first question. The first child to raise his hand is allowed to answer. If he is right, he wins a prize. If wrong, pick another child to answer.

Repeat until all questions have been answered.

● **START**

PLAYING

Time the children to see who can say all the commandments the fastest. If you have a large number of children participating, have your workers divide them into groups and assist you. Award prizes and praise to winners.

This game is best played after you have completed the **Power Tool Box** unit on the Ten Commandments where the kids learned a "secret code" to help them memorize the commandments. If you would like to get a copy of this "secret code," give us a call...for the right price, we'll let you in on the secret!

Ten Commandment Memory Game

PROPS: Stopwatch and bag of prizes.

PARTICIPANTS: All children who can say the Ten Commandments.

● **START** -

PROPS: 2 8-foot-long tables, 10 plastic bowling pins and 2 pumpkins (or large round melons).

PARTICIPANTS: 2 teams of 2 (1 bowler and 1 catcher).

YOU ARE HERE

Set the tables end to end. Put the pumpkins on one end, the pins on the other end. Have the bowler from the first team stand next to the pumpkins while his teammate, the catcher, stands near the pins. Have the bowler roll the first pumpkin down the tables to see how many pins he can knock over.

The catcher must catch the pumpkin before it hits the floor, but he must not bump the table. Repeat the action with the second pumpkin. Count how many pins the bowler knocked down. Subtract one point for each time the catcher failed to catch the pumpkin before it hit the floor. Then let the other team play the game. The team with the most points is the winner.

Be sure to remove any stems from the fruit you will be rolling. Also make sure your floors are protected in case a pumpkin or melon fall and break open. You may wish to fold the legs of your table and place the tables directly on the floor.

● **START**

Write one letter of the word "forgiveness" on each sheet of paper. Make two sets.

Give each letter holder one letter to hold. Let both Super Spellers look at the word so they know how to spell it. Then turn the Super Spellers around and scramble the letter holders.

When you say "Go," the Super Spellers must unscramble their teammates to correctly spell "forgiveness." The first one to spell it correctly wins.

Be sure the letters are big enough to be seen by everyone. Also, be sure the holders are holding the letters so that they can be easily seen.

Super Spellers

PROPS: Marker and 22 sheets of construction paper.

PARTICIPANTS: 1 boy and 1 girl to be "Super Spellers." A group of 11 boys and a group of 11 girls to be letter holders.

● **START**

PROPS: 4 hula hoops and children's praise cassette.

PARTICIPANTS: 2 boys and 2 girls.

This will be a contest to see who can keep a hula hoop spinning around her waist for the longest time. Give each kid a hula hoop. When you start the music, they start spinning the hoops around themselves. Keep the music playing until all the hula hoops have fallen to the floor. You might choose to play the game two or three times. If you have more hula hoops, add more participants to make it more exciting.

Let the kids practice the hula hoop game for a minute or two. The better they play, the more entertaining this game will be.

● **START**

Scripture Drill

PROPS: 2 Bibles

PARTICIPANTS: 1 boy, 1 girl and leader.

Both children must stand in front of the group with a closed Bible in hand. The leader calls out a pre-planned Scripture reference. The children immediately start searching for the verse. The first to find it raises his hand. The leader calls out "stop," and the child must then read the verse aloud. If it is the correct verse, a point is given. If it is wrong, let them both continue searching. Repeat this process using five different verses from both the Old and New Testament. The child with the highest score wins.

Beware of calling out confusing sounding Scripture references that will be difficult to remember while searching.

YOU ARE HERE

 **START**

Balloon Blastin' Dart Toss

PROPS: Tape, 20 balloons, large board and 5 darts.

PARTICIPANTS: 4 children— 2 for each team.

PLAYING

Tape inflated balloons to the board and set it at or above eye level for the participants. Allow the smaller kids on each team to be the first participants. Each kid has five throws with the darts and scores are combined for a team total.

If there is a tie, have a "pop-off." The first one to pop a balloon in the pop-off will win.

 **HINT**

Be sure that no one is in or near the line of fire.

YOU ARE HERE

● START

YOU ARE HERE

Batter Up

PROPS: Oversized plastic bat, ten water balloons and baseball home plate.

PARTICIPANTS: 1 boy, 1 girl and 2 adults (one to pitch and one to act as the catcher/umpire).

Have the first child stand beside home plate with the bat. The pitcher tosses the first water balloon (underhand), and the batter tries to hit it. The catcher/umpire calls the strikes and balls. If the pitcher throws a ball, the batter will get another chance. Each batter has at least three chances. Score points as follows:

-If the pitch was a strike, the child will get zero points.

-If the batter hits the ball but it doesn't break, she scores one point.

-If the batter hits and breaks the ball, she earns two points.

Ten balloons will provide you with two extras for accidental breakage or a tie. Balloons need to be the same size and big enough to pop with the bat. They must not be so big that they will pop every time. Place a plastic drop cloth (or tarp) under the batter.

● **START** - - - - - - - - - - - - - - - - - -

I'm Forever Blowing Bubbles

PROPS: 6 small bottles of bubble solution with wands and stopwatch (or watch with second hand).

PARTICIPANTS: 6 children.

Have the kids come to the front of the room and stand in a line, facing the rest of the children. Give them each a bottle of bubble solution, and tell them to carefully open the bottles and take out the wand. Instruct them to not blow any bubbles until you count to three. Tell them the object of the game is to see who can blow the biggest bubble in 30 seconds. Have your KIDS Church watch to see who blows the biggest bubble while you time 30 seconds. At the end of the time, tell the participants to stop. The boy or girl who blew the biggest bubble is the winner! Let the six players take their bubble solution home with them.

▼ **HINT**

Bubble solution will sting eyes, so tell the kids to keep it away from their eyes. If some bubble solution gets into a child's eyes, have a worker ready to take the child to a sink and rinse his eyes with water. Also, if bubble solution gets spilled on the carpet, rinse thoroughly with water and dry with towel.

● **START**

PLAYING

YOU ARE HERE

Frisbee® Toss

PROPS: 2 Frisbees®.

PARTICIPANTS: 2 boys and 2 girls, 2 adult workers (1 for each team). The adults will serve as runners to return the Frisbees®.

The boy stands on the front row on one of the sides; the girl stands on the front row of the other side. The two other kids will stand on the stage, each holding a Frisbee®. On the count of three, the kids on the stage toss their Frisbees® to their team-mates. The catchers are not to move their feet. If both sides catch the Frisbee®, they will move back to the second row. The Frisbees® will be returned by the runners to the kids on the stage, who will repeat the toss. The game keeps repeating with the boy and girl moving back another row at each toss until one misses.

● **START**

PREP

YOU ARE HERE

Paint the tires, tie them together and suspend them from the ceiling.

Note: Cardboard with cut-out targets can be substituted for the tires.

PLAYING

Have the first boy and girl stand about 20 feet from the target. They both try to throw a softball (underhand) through the tire opening. If they make it through, their team earns one point. The second boy and girl come forward to repeat the process.

The first and second players alternate until each has completed five throws. The team with the most points is the winner.

HINT

Set the game in a protected area. Have one or two helpers retrieve and return the balls quickly to keep the game moving along.

Softball Shoot

PROPS: Paint, rope, 3 old tires and 4 softballs.

PARTICIPANTS: 2 boys, 2 girls and 2 helpers.

● **START**

YOU ARE HERE

Stack the cans in two pyramids—each stack has three on the bottom, two in the middle and one on top. Set the pyramids on the stage.

The participants should each stand at the same distance from the stacks. They will take three tennis balls each and throw them at the pyramids. The one with the fewest cans standing is the winner.

Soda Can Pyramid

PROPS: 6 tennis balls and 12 soda cans.

PARTICIPANTS: 1 boy and 1 girl.

● **START**

YOU ARE HERE

Set up the bowling pins in the standard position, about 20 feet from the two players.

The participants each get to throw two Frisbees® to see how many pins they can knock down. Whoever knocks down the most pins wins.

Frisbee® Bowling

PROPS: 2 Frisbees® and 1 set of plastic bowling pins.

PARTICIPANTS: 1 boy and 1 girl.

● **START**

YOU ARE HERE

Bible Basketball

PROPS: 2 small basketballs, 2 small basketball hoops, plywood and pole.

PARTICIPANTS: 2 children and 2 helpers.

Attach basketball hoops side by side to a backboard made of plywood. The backboard and hoops need to be placed on a pole or beam so it stands about seven feet from floor.

Have the participants stand an equal distance from the backboard. Give them one minute to see who can get the most basketballs in the hoop. With each basket scored, the child must call out the name of a book of the Bible in order for the basket to count. Book may not be repeated. Have the helpers retrieve the balls for the kids. Make sure the participants' feet don't move.

Try the game out beforehand in order to figure out the best distance for the kids to stand from the backboard. Make sure someone keeps track of all the books which have been named.

● **START**

YOU ARE HERE

PLAYING

Ring Fling

PROPS: 2 plastic swords (or broom handles/dowels) and 10 embroidery hoops (or rings made from stiff rope secured with duct tape).

PARTICIPANTS: 2 boys and 2 girls.

Each team has a catcher and a thrower. The catchers stand back to back, each of them holding a sword. The throwers both stand an equal distance away from their partners. They will throw one ring at a time to their partners, who will try to catch the rings with their swords. The catchers can move their swords but not their feet. The team which catches the most rings is the winner.

HINT

The distance the throwers stand from the catchers is important. The game should be neither too easy nor too hard.

● **START** - - - - - - - - - - - - - - - - - -

YOU
ARE
HERE

PREP

Pie-In-the-Face

PROPS: 6 9-inch aluminum disposable pie tins, 2 cans of shaving cream, 3 bath towels, chair, masking tape and plastic trash bags (or plastic).

PARTICIPANTS: 6 children.

Have a worker load the pie tins with shaving cream about 4-5 inches high. Set the chair at the front of the room with plastic or trash bags to protect the room. Place a masking tape line on the floor about 8 feet from the chair.

PLAYING

Have your worker organize the six children in a single file line behind the masking tape. You sit in the chair. Put a bath towel around your shoulders to cover your upper body. When everyone is ready, your worker will give the first shaving cream pie to the first child in line. Each participant will get a chance to toss one pie at you.

HINT

Be sure to keep your eyes closed and free from shaving cream. It will sting your eyes. However, shaving cream is much easier to clean up than any other pie filling. If you wear glasses, remove them before undergoing this ordeal. Have one of your workers standing by you with a towel to wipe your eyes if necessary.

● **START**

YOU ARE HERE

PLAYING

Have the kids take turns trying to kick or toss the ball into a garbage can. Let each participant try two times. The team that kicks the ball into the can the most times is the winner.

HINT

Plan this game according to your kids' church setup. Take appropriate safety precautions.

● **START**

Pizza Pitchin'

PROPS: 2 Frisbees®, 2 pizza boxes and stopwatch.

PARTICIPANTS: 2 teams of 2 kids each and 2 helpers.

Assign a boy from one team and a girl from the other to be the "pizza catchers." Give them each a pizza box and have them face the audience. The other two players are the "pizza pitchers." Give them each a Frisbee® and have them stand 10-12 feet in front of their partners.

When you say "Go," the pitchers throw their Frisbees® into the pizza box, and the catchers try to close their boxes on the Frisbees® and "catch" them. Have a helper on each team quickly retrieve the Frisbee® and get it back to the pitcher so they can toss it again. The helper will also keep score for the team they're helping. The team catching the most Frisbees® in 90 seconds wins.

● **START**

YOU ARE HERE

PLAYING

I Wish I Had a Helmet

PROPS: 2 working squirt guns, 2 candles and matches.

PARTICIPANTS: 4 children.

Divide the four kids into two teams. Have two of the kids face the audience and give them a lit candle to hold in front of their faces. Caution them not to blow out the candles. Put the other two kids on their knees with the squirt gun about 5-7 feet in front of their teammates. When you say "Go," they need to try to put out the candle with the squirt gun. All the kids will laugh as they see the kids holding the candles getting drenched. The first team to put the candle out wins.

HINT

Be sure both squirt guns work and are comparable in shooting strength and accuracy. Have two of your helpers watch to make sure the candles do not burn anyone's hair. If you are uncomfortable with allowing the kids to get wet, have them wear plastic trash can liners with holes cut out for their heads and arms.

● START

YOU ARE HERE

PLAYING

Water Balloon Shave

PROPS: 2 water balloons covered with shaving cream and 2 hand razors for shaving (medium sharp).

PARTICIPANTS: 4 kids divided into 2 teams.

One kid from each team is seated in a chair facing the audience. With one hand, his partner, "the shaver," holds the creamed balloon over the head of the one seated. Set the time for two minutes. On the word "Go," using his free hand, "the shaver" must carefully shave the balloon. The first to break the balloon is out. If neither balloon breaks after two minutes, the one who has shaved the most cream off the balloon wins.

HINT

Advise the kids sitting in the chairs to keep their eyes closed. The balloon may pop at any time and shaving cream will fly. Have towels on hand.

START

YOU ARE HERE

PLAYING

PROPS: 4 regular squirt guns, 32 feet (or longer) of rope, 4 western hats (optional), stopwatch (or watch with second hand) and towels.

PARTICIPANTS: 8 children.

Give fully loaded squirt guns to four of the children and tell them to hold them between their knees until you say, "Go!" Give them each a western hat to wear on their heads. Form the other four children into an 8-foot square, each at one corner, and wrap the rope around the outside of the children forming a square. This will make your "corral." Then, tell the four with the water guns to go into the "OK Corral." Tell them they are going to have a "Wild West Water Pistol Squirt Down at the OK Corral!" The object of the game is to be the first to empty the squirt gun. The first to raise an empty gun is the winner. Shout, "GO!"

Give them towels to dry off.

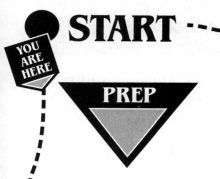

START

YOU ARE HERE

PREP

Speedy Sponge Relay

PROPS: 6 large sponges, 2 pails and 2 2-liter clear plastic soda bottles.

PARTICIPANTS: 2 teams (3 boys compete with 3 girls).

Fill pails with water. Remove the labels from bottles and cut off the top sections (four inches from top). Place the two pails of water at the back of the room.

PLAYING

A player for each team takes a sponge and begins soaking it in the pail prior to the "Go" command. On the "Go" command, the players run their water-soaked sponges to the front and wring them into their teams' bottles. They run back to tag the next players to repeat the process. Players can be soaking their sponges while awaiting their turns.

Set a time limit of two or three minutes for the relay. The winning team is determined by the volume of water in the bottles.

HINT

Consider the floor surface and keep the playing area safe. Have clean-up towels available for spills.

START

PLAYING

Team Water Works

PROPS: 2 pails filled with water, 8 paper cups, long table (or 2 tables), plastic table covering, floor covering and 2 clear, empty soda bottles.

PARTICIPANTS: 4 boys and 4 girls.

Place the table in the middle of the stage. Put the two empty soda bottles toward the middle of the table, one for each team. Have both teams stand behind the table, facing the audience. Have the boys line up on the right side of the table, and the girls line up on the left side.

Place the pails of water on the floor at each end. Give each player a paper cup. The object of the game is to relay the water from the bucket to the soda bottle, a cup at a time. When you say "Go," the players stationed by the pails dip their cups and then pour the water into the next teammates' cup. They repeat the process, pouring their water into the third players' cup and so on until the last player pours the water into the soda bottles. The teams do not have to wait for the first cup of water to go down the line and into the bottle before they start a second cup. The first team to fill the bottle is the winner.

HINT

If you use large bottles, draw a line on the bottles for a finish line.